Dave -
Just
old - times

Love,
Mom

MW00695647

Just Sons

The Mischief, Mayhem and Marvel of Boys

BY MELISSA SOVEY

▧ WILLOW CREEK PRESS®

Published by Willow Creek Press, Inc.
P.O. Box 147, Minocqua, Wisconsin 54548

Photo Credits:

p6 © AlaskaStock/Masterfile; p9 © Mike & Lisa Husar/www.teamhusar.com;
p13,14,17 © Mike & Lisa Husar/www.teamhusar.com; p18 © Klein-Hubert/www.kimballstock.com;
p21 © Visuals Unlimited/Masterfile; p22 © Minden Pictures/Masterfile;
p25 © Mike & Lisa Husar/www.teamhusar.com; p26 © Minden Pictures/Masterfile;
p29 © Tom & Pat Leeson/www.kimballstock.com; p30 © Cusp and Flirt/Masterfile;
p33 © Daniel J. Cox/www.kimballstock.com; p34 © Klein-Hubert/www.kimballstock.com;
p37 © Minden Pictures/Masterfile; p38 © Lynn M. Stone/www.kimballstock.com;
p41 © F. Lukasseck/Masterfile; p42 © Mike & Lisa Husar/www.teamhusar.com;
p46 © Rommel/Masterfile; p49,50 © Mike & Lisa Husar/www.teamhusar.com;
p53 © Minden Pictures/Masterfile; p54 © Mike & Lisa Husar/www.teamhusar.com;
p57 © Minden Pictures/Masterfile; p58 © Tom & Pat Leeson/www.kimballstock.com;
p61 © Minden Pictures/Masterfile; p62 © Cultura RM/Masterfile; p65 © ClassicStock/Masterfile;
p66 © Gloria H. Chomica/Masterfile; p69 © Gary Gerovac/Masterfile;
p70, 73 © Mike & Lisa Husar/www.teamhusar.com; p74 © Minden Pictures/Masterfile;
p77 © Thomas Kitchin & Vict/www.agefotostock.com; p78 © Denver Bryan/www.kimballstock.com;
p81,85, 86 © Mike & Lisa Husar/www.teamhusar.com; p89 © AlaskaStock/Masterfile;
p90 © Mike & Lisa Husar/www.teamhusar.com; p93 © Wildlife Bildagentur GmbH/www.kimballstock.com;
p94 © Mike & Lisa Husar/www.teamhusar.com

Design: Donnie Rubo
Printed in Canada

What are little boys made of?
Snips and snails
And puppy dogs' tails,
That's what little boys are made of.

For my sons, Michael, Parker and Drew and my grandson,
Kaeden (who just needed a little extra puppy dog tail that day).

You are the lights of my life.

A FEW FACTS ABOUT BOYS

Boy, *n*.: a noise with dirt on it.

—*Not Your Average Dictionary*

"Boys are beyond the range of anybody's sure understanding, at least when they are between the ages of 18 months and 90 years."

—*James Thurber*

"Conscience: That which makes a boy tell his mother before his sister does."

—*Laurence J. Peter*

"A small son can charm himself into,
and out of, most things."

—*Jenny de Vries*

"A boy is naturally full of humor."

—*Robert Baden-Powell*

"Of all the animals, the boy is the most unmanageable."

—*Plato*

"A characteristic of the normal child is
he doesn't act that way very often."

—*Author Unknown*

"Never underestimate a child's ability to get into more trouble."

—*Martin Mull*

"A fairly bright boy is far more intelligent and far better company than the average adult."

—*John B.S. Haldane*

"Boys wear their hearts on their sleeves. Even when they're trying to pull one over on you they're so transparent. Like men."

—*Patricia Heaton*

"Boys do not grow up gradually. They move forward in spurts like the hands of clocks in railway stations."

—*Cyril Connolly*

IN THE BEGINNING...
BABIES AND BOYHOOD

"The child must know that he is a miracle,
that since the beginning of the world there
hasn't been, and until the end of the world
there will not be, another child like him."

—*Pablo Casals*

"A boy's story is the best that is ever told."

—*Charles Dickens*

"Whenever I held my newborn baby in my arms, I used to think that what I said and did to him could have an influence not only on him but on all whom he met, not only for a day or a month or a year, but for all eternity—a very challenging and exciting thought for a mother."

—*Rose Kennedy*

"You are worried about seeing him spend his early years in doing nothing. What! Is it nothing to be happy? Nothing to skip, play, and run around all day long? Never in his life will he be so busy again."

—Jean-Jacques Rousseau

"A young child is, indeed, a true scientist, just one big question mark. What? Why? How? I never cease to marvel at the recurring miracle of growth, to be fascinated by the mystery and wonder of this brave enthusiasm."

—*Victoria Wagner*

"Oh, for boyhood's painless play, sleep that wakes in laughing day, health that mocks the doctor's rules, knowledge never learned of schools."

—*John Greenleaf Whittier*

"Children's games are hardly games. Children are never more serious than when they play."

—*Montaigne*

"My father used to play with my brother and me in the yard. Mother would come out and say, 'You're tearing up the grass.' 'We're not raising grass,' Dad would reply. 'We're raising boys.'"

—*Harmon Killebrew*

"Loving a child doesn't mean giving in to all his whims; to love him is to bring out the best in him, to teach him to love what is difficult."

—*Nadia Boulanger*

"Listen to the MUSTN'TS, child, listen to the DON'TS. Listen to the SHOULDN'TS, the IMPOSSIBLES, the WON'TS. Listen to the NEVER HAVES then listen close to me—anything can happen, child, ANYTHING can be."

—*Shel Silverstein*

"If you can give your son or daughter only one gift, let it be Enthusiasm."

—*Bruce Barton*

LESSONS FROM OUR SONS

"We learn courageous action by going
forward whenever fear urges us back.
A little boy was asked how he learned
to skate. 'By getting up every time
I fell down,' he answered."

—*David Seabury*

"My sons have been my finest teachers and my greatest sources of joy. They have given me courage and strength when I worried I would have none; we have always been a team."

—*Melissa Sovey*

"It is not flesh and blood, but heart which makes us fathers and sons."

—*Friedrich von Schiller*

"If you think there are no new frontiers, watch a boy ring the front doorbell on his first date."

—Olin Miller

"When a father gives to his son, both laugh;
when a son gives to his father, both cry."

—*William Shakespeare*

"How beautiful is youth! How bright
it gleams with its illusions,
aspirations, dreams!"

—*Henry Wadsworth Longfellow*

"The priceless treasure of boyhood is
his endless enthusiasm, his high store
of idealism, his affections and his hopes.
When we preserve these, we have
made men. We have made citizens
and we have made Americans."

—*Herbert Clark Hoover*

TURNING POINTS...
INTO ADOLESCENCE

"If you want to recapture your
youth, just cut off his allowance."

—Al Bernstein

"Consider the postage stamp, my son. It secures success through its ability to stick to one thing till it gets there."

—*Josh Billings*

"Rule of thumb for feeding teenage boys: For every two boys, quadruple the amount of food you think you should have on hand."

—*Melissa Sovey*

"Boyhood is the longest time in life for a boy. The last term of the school-year is made of decades, not of weeks, and living through them is like waiting for the millennium."

—*Booth Tarkington*

"If you can keep your wits about you while all others are losing theirs, and blaming you. The world will be yours and everything in it, what's more, you'll be a man, my son."

—*Rudyard Kipling*

"A boy becomes an adult three years before his parents think he does, and about two years after he thinks he does."

—*Lewis B. Hershey*

"Wherever they go, and whatever happens to them on the way, in that enchanted place on the top of the forest, a little boy and his Bear will always be playing."

—A.A. Milne

AND NOW YOU ARE GROWN

"Tall oaks from little acorns grow."

—*David Everett*

"A child enters your home and for the next twenty years makes so much noise you can hardly stand it. The child departs, leaving the house so silent you think you are going mad."

—*John Andrew Holmes*

"Your children tell you casually years later what it would have killed you with worry to know at the time."

—*Mignon McLaughlin*

"When you have brought up kids, there are memories you store directly in your tear ducts."

—*Robert Brault*

"You don't raise heroes; you raise sons. And if you treat them like sons, they'll turn out to be heroes, even if it's just in your own eyes."

—*Walter Schirra Sr.*

"There is no miraculous change that takes place in a boy that makes him a man. He becomes a man by being a man."

—Louis L'Amour

"The true wealth of a nation lies not in its gold or silver but in its learning, wisdom, and in the uprightness of its sons."

—*Kahlil Gibran*

"Unless artists can remember what it was to be a little boy, they are only half complete as artist and as man."

—*James Thurber*

"It is a great moment in life when a father sees a son grow taller than he or reach farther."

—*Richard L. Evans*

"If I have a monument in this world, it is my son."

—*Maya Angelou*